T0414216

Fungi

by Brienna Rossiter

FOCUS
READERS®
BEACON

www.focusreaders.com

Focus Readers is distributed by North Star Editions:
sales@northstareditions.com | 888-417-0195

Produced for Focus Readers by Red Line Editorial.

Photographs ©: Shutterstock Images, cover, 1, 4, 8, 10, 12, 14, 17, 27; iStockphoto, 7, 18, 22, 29; Andreas Mallinckrodt/Alamy, 20; Alessandro Dahan/Getty Images News/Getty Images, 24

Library of Congress Cataloging-in-Publication Data
Names: Rossiter, Brienna, author.
Title: Fungi / by Brienna Rossiter.
Description: Mendota Heights, MN: Focus Readers, [2025] | Series: Decomposers | Includes index. | Audience: Grades 2-3
Identifiers: LCCN 2024023660 (print) | LCCN 2024023661 (ebook) | ISBN 9798889983989 (hardcover) | ISBN 9798889984269 (paperback) | ISBN 9798889984801 (pdf) | ISBN 9798889984542 (ebook)
Subjects: LCSH: Fungi--Juvenile literature.
Classification: LCC QK603.5 .R65 2025 (print) | LCC QK603.5 (ebook) | DDC 579.5--dc23/eng/20240607
LC record available at https://lccn.loc.gov/2024023660
LC ebook record available at https://lccn.loc.gov/2024023661

Printed in the United States of America
Mankato, MN
012025

About the Author

Brienna Rossiter is a writer and editor who lives in Minnesota.

Table of Contents

CHAPTER 1

In the Forest

A fallen tree lies in the forest. Mushrooms grow along its trunk. They break down the wood. Over time, the wood becomes soft. It starts to crumble.

 **Fungi can take years to break down dead trees.**

Small bits of wood drop off the trunk. They fall to the forest floor. Young plants grow in this rich soil.

Other fungi live under the dirt. These fungi send out thread-like shoots. Some shoots help the fungi take in **nutrients**. Other shoots link

Did You Know?

Some types of fungi can grow several feet wide. Other fungi are tiny. Yeast is one example. It is made of just one **cell**. People need microscopes to see it.

together. The long threads form **networks**. Fungi networks are a key part of forest life. They connect to many plants.

CHAPTER 2

Breaking It Down

Ecosystems have three kinds of living things. Producers make their own food. Consumers eat other living things. And decomposers get energy by breaking things down. Fungi are a type of decomposer.

 **Fungi live all around the world. They can survive almost anywhere.**

Fungi are a **kingdom** of living things. This kingdom includes mushrooms, yeasts, and rusts. Mildews, smuts, and molds are fungi, too.

Fungi break down plants and animals. A fungus does this by growing on something. Then the fungus releases enzymes. They break things down into smaller parts. The fungus takes these tiny bits into its body.

This process impacts ecosystems in many ways. It keeps dead things from piling up. It also helps gases and nutrients move between organisms. As fungi break down things, chemicals are released.

> Some mushrooms can be eaten. For example, many people eat truffles.

Some chemicals come from the things being decomposed. Other chemicals are created by the fungi. These chemicals go into the soil, air, or water.

Some chemicals are important nutrients. Other living things need them to live and grow. Fungi free the chemicals for plants and animals to use. This process is called nutrient cycling.

Fungi are also part of the carbon cycle. Plants and animals are made partly of a substance called carbon. As fungi break them down, the carbon is let out.

Did You Know?

People use some fungi to make food. Bread and cheese are two examples.

CHAPTER 3

Tons of Fungi

Earth has many types of fungi. They live in a wide variety of places. Some live in soil. Others live in air or water. Most fungi break down dead things. This process spreads nutrients.

 **Scientists have found more than 100,000 kinds of fungi. But millions of kinds likely exist.**

Nitrogen is one example. Plants need this nutrient to grow and live. The breakdown process adds nitrogen back to the soil.

Other fungi grow on plants or animals that are still living. The fungi can grow inside them, too. Some of these fungi harm the organisms. Some fungi make people or animals sick. But others hurt plants. For example, fungi cause Dutch elm disease. This disease has killed many trees.

Cordyceps are fungi that take over an animal's brain and feed on its body.

Fungi can also harm crops. If fungi spread quickly, people can run out of food.

However, many fungi team up with other organisms in helpful ways. Lichen is one example. It is a mix of algae and fungi. They grow together. They also share nutrients. The fungi take in water. And the algae make food.

Other fungi grow on plant roots. The fungi help plants get nutrients from the soil. Then the plants can make energy. The plants share this energy with the fungi.

Did You Know?

Many fungi spread by sending out spores. Spores float through the air. They land in a new place and grow there.

CHAPTER 4

Underground Networks

The main part of a fungus is usually underground. Fungi are made of strands called hyphae. These strands look like white threads. They can stretch far.

 **A fairy ring may form when one underground fungus sends many parts above ground.**

 About 75 percent of Earth's carbon is stored below ground. Mycorrhizal fungi help plants take in carbon.

And they can join together. Many form large networks.

Fungi networks often connect to plants. Mycorrhizal fungi are an example. They grow on tree roots. They help trees take in water, carbon, and **minerals**. They also connect trees together. The trees can share water or other nutrients.

Fungi team up with bacteria, too. They may share nutrients. Fungi also help some bacteria move. The bacteria travel along the fungi's threads.

Fungi networks are a key part of healthy ecosystems. They help soil stay balanced. For example, too much nitrogen can harm plants.

Some fungi can take in nitrogen. They use it to make protein. By doing this, they remove nitrogen from soil.

Some types of fungi let out **greenhouse gases** when breaking things down. These gases cause

climate change. However, many types of fungi store carbon. They help lessen climate change. But fungi can break easily. People can hurt fungi networks when building or farming. That lets out carbon. Protecting these fungi helps Earth stay healthy.

Did You Know?

Some fungi live in animals' stomachs. They help the animals **digest** food.

Controlling Carbon

Trees take in carbon from the air. They use it to make energy. As they grow, carbon gets trapped in their wood. It stays out of the air.

Mycorrhizal fungi help trees grow faster and store more carbon. So, healthy forests and fungi protect the planet. However, pollution can kill fungi. For example, many farms use fertilizer. It helps plants grow. But it often gets into nearby soil. It can kill fungi. To stop this problem, people are trying new ways of farming. One way uses fungi. The fungi help plants get nutrients. That way, plants don't need fertilizer.

Fertilizer often has high levels of nitrogen. If too much of this chemical gets into soil, it kills fungi.

Focus Questions

Write your answers on a separate piece of paper.

1. Write a sentence describing one way fungi help ecosystems stay balanced.

2. Which fact about fungi did you find most interesting? Why?

3. How do decomposers get energy?
   - **A.** by producing their own food
   - **B.** by hunting other living things
   - **C.** by breaking things down

4. What might happen to plants if fungi did not exist?
   - **A.** Animals would eat all the plants.
   - **B.** Plants wouldn't take in enough nutrients.
   - **C.** Plants would grow much bigger.

5. What does **impacts** mean in this book?

*This process **impacts** ecosystems in many ways. It keeps dead things from piling up. It also helps gases and nutrients move between organisms.*

    A. has an effect on
    B. stays away from
    C. is not part of

6. What does **variety** mean in this book?

*They live in a wide **variety** of places. Some live in soil. Others live in air or water.*

    A. a single type
    B. a large range
    C. a dry area

Answer key on page 32.

Glossary

cell
The smallest unit of a living organism that can function and perform tasks.

climate change
A human-caused global crisis involving long-term changes in Earth's temperature and weather patterns.

digest
To break down food so it can be used by the body.

ecosystems
The collections of living things in different natural areas.

greenhouse gases
Gases that trap heat in Earth's atmosphere, causing climate change.

kingdom
One of the large groups that all life-forms are divided into. Examples include plants, animals, and fungi.

minerals
Substances that form naturally under the ground.

networks
Groups of things that are connected together.

nutrients
Substances that living things need to stay strong and healthy.

To Learn More

BOOKS

Huddleston, Emma. *Decomposers and Scavengers: Nature's Recyclers*. Minneapolis: Abdo Publishing, 2020.

Loh-Hagan, Virginia. *Weird Science: Plants and Fungi*. Ann Arbor, MI: Cherry Lake Publishing, 2021.

Rosenberg, Pam. *Gross Stuff Underground*. Mankato, MN: The Child's World, 2021.

NOTE TO EDUCATORS

Visit **www.focusreaders.com** to find lesson plans, activities, links, and other resources related to this title.

Index